Breath

Robert VanderMolen

New Issues Poetry & Prose

A Green Rose Book
Selected by Herbert Scott

New Issues Poetry & Prose
The College of Arts and Sciences
Western Michigan University
Kalamazoo, Michigan 49008

An Inland Seas Poetry Book

 Inland Seas poetry books are supported by a grant from The Michigan Council for Arts and Cultural Affairs.

Copyright© 2000 by Robert VanderMolen. All rights reserved.
Printed in the United States of America.

First Edition, 2000.

ISBN: 0-932826-97-0 (paperbound)

Library of Congress Cataloging-in-Publication Data:
VanderMolen, Robert
Breath/Robert VanderMolen
Library of Congress Catalog Card Number (99-76776)

Art Direction:	Tricia Hennessy
Design:	Jason Maliszewski
Production:	Paul Sizer
	The Design Center, Department of Art
	College of Fine Arts
	Western Michigan University
Printing:	Courier Corporation

Breath

Robert VanderMolen

New Issues
WESTERN MICHIGAN UNIVERSITY

Also by Robert VanderMolen

Peaches
Along the River
Circumstances
The Pavilion

for Deb

Contents

Cricket Poem	3
The Brightness	7
Bodies	8
Detail	9
Showtime	10
Monotony	13
Heather	15
A New Restaurant	16
The New Neighbors	18
Diebenkorn's *Ocean Park #52*	20
Saturday	21
Birds Too	22
Accountability	24
Two Parts	26
Coasts	28
A Town on the River	30
Hairbrush	32
Flies	33
The Snakes	34
Brick	35
The Focus	37
Night	38
Philip	40
Families	42
Outside of Town	44
Up North	45
In May	46
Veterans	48
The Cottonwoods	49
Summer of '94	50
Breath	52
Hired Hand	54
Beetles	55
Neighbors	56
Once	57
Elm Ridge Street	58
The Painting	60

Cricket Poem

She said I could borrow crickets
For my bedroom

We had met in line at the post office
We were wearing similar shirts

She said she would cook
Abalone that I would dive for
And that her bedroom faced
The ocean

We walked towards her cottage

Mine
Grins into the woods I said
And I've dusted the bust of my grandfather
The moon is polite there

She nodded
Then said
That her crickets were
The best in the country

We were now in her kitchen

I said I hope
That they are not spoiled

To which she kissed me quickly
And said you certainly are
A darling
And I will always love you

And she undressed
And I gazed partly over the ocean

Breath

The Brightness

As an older frame house, a large one,
Moves slowly down the road on wheels
It isolates a cross-cut breeze.
Everyone stops talking, the laundry sheets
Clap—how daytime slips off
the magazine page into something
like erotica.
How the tide muscles in
While you're asleep, basking on a rock
40 yards from shore.
After torpor, days watching predictable insects.
Rudy's Meat Market, that landmark, razed while we were dozing
(turned into a modern bank—where for awhile the tellers
seemed like waitresses). Or the hardware store
Transformed to sell pizzas. The sky pelting rain,
Size of bullets. The trolley tracks submerge
Half-way through the intersection. The cemetery to the right
So accustomed to being there—while everything crept west
including the cold house pulled by truck. Birds too.
As the wave smacks a jetty, out of the mulling nowhere
Just you, waving a flute
Farther west than anyone you knew. In that pause
Where one decade blots out another in the popular mind—
revisionists always have their work.
Sooner or later water leaves the intersection
High tide marks on light poles. The gas station manager
Retethers his monkey to the square campus of grass.
The girls return. Well, temporarily.
Magazines in hand.
A funeral procession angles into the mural.
There's a drunk over the curb with out-of-state plates.
Crowds that gather at police road-blocks
The panicked cemetery deer

Events are half-motion, half-real.
One stares 40 years from shore
Or from the concrete of a traffic island—
here or not here. That ocean of sound
Retreating into idleness, dread or wonder

One opts for wonder

Bodies

This boy came into the library
Said there was a body
In the river.
I didn't just fall off
A turnip truck, she said.
Being originally from Saginaw
Or Bad Ax . . .
One cold front following another
Week after week.
The weatherman answers his door
With a pistol stuck in the elastic
Of his jogging pants.
I know a drunk when I sleep
With one, she continued.
He used to ski too
Until the cold got him.
But he wasn't no suicide.
Not in his family. They like to fight.
The attorney removed his glasses.
The older you get
The worse you look without money.
On TV a documentary
Pointed out that ancient columns
Were modeled on tree trunks.
Maybe they ran out
Of large trees. I don't know,
She said, everytime you get one thing
Figured out . . .

Detail

Someone looking
Remarkably like George Simenon
In the shadow, with pipe lit
As the body of a young woman
From a tenement off Franklin
Is hauled to the street—who'd
had a bottle shoved in her
and cracked off—under a hat
Like a newspaperman, say
In the 50's, notebook in hand.
Almost bemused, fascinated by what
He'd be allowed to learn later—
despite a whiff of anger
a breeze burning out an alley—
Depredations less odious the farther
One retreated from the valley—
a city map or two from Orchard
Country, those apple-faced
innocents content with ponds and ridges.
Truth was, everyone from the coroner
To the judge to the editor
Knew they had better secrets
Than anyone else, save the old industrialists—
at poker, a phrase or two was worth mountains
of detail, seasons of minutia, filing cabinets
packed inside filing cabinets—
Hunger working for its own sake.
A nod in the right direction
Kept orchards stretching to the Straits

Showtime

    I.
Showtime, says the dentist.
He flicks on lights for the x-rays.
I liked it better
When they were more serious
Or if when they joked
It was closer to family humor.
An uncle at Thanksgiving
Who'd lived in Europe when young.

    That polished scent of lumber-boom wood

Up the middle
Of the white anvil building on the corner . . .

    II.
A block past the newspaper offices
A Plymouth Stationwagon
Was suspended in a Department Store glass entrance—
This modern enclosure 3 stories high.
I marveled.
We were briskly out of the war years
Though I didn't realize
That was what the excitement was about

    Dad bought a similar stationwagon
Only it didn't have wooden panels on the sides

By the time I was 14
We had boards on the floors so our feet wouldn't fall through

The heater didn't work
And one warm spring day
When the vent was opened
The car filled with bees

III.
My doctor, a serene detective type,
Smoked cigars
Never seemed discouraged by my illnesses

A burly man, humming to himself, he occupied
A squat turn-of-the-century building
At the edge of the red-light district

*   *   *

There was an ex-boxer
Who let us sit on his porch
His daughter was a hooker
We pissed in his tub with him when the toilet was jammed . . .

*   *   *

Or my Dad and I
Throwing stones in the river
We'd taken from a planter inside the bank.
That sky pebbled with noon

*   *   *

My grandmother saying, as I sat down for lunch,
At the Juvenile Home
Boys don't have much choice in their education.
But she worked there.
I drove her when I was older.
I also heard the tale
That they screwed through the fence
(Separating the sexes)
The girls backing up in a knot,
Their pants down, to the metal diamonds of cross-hatching

IV.

My brother and I sat playing

In sand under sassafras. You look up
And watch a city bus crunching into a parked car.

Or boys hunted by men, escaping into woodlots.
Men once ran through the roads we were constructing.
Large flat footprints.
Police cars converging
On a street of empty warehouses

V.
Or when the President addressed the populous.
Faces
Without mouths

Men in dark suits
On top of buildings with rifles

Monotony

1.
The shadow over my bunk
Looked like a breast,
A small breast, with pronounced nipple

    Behind the stove
Necklaces of spider-webs
Bark and lint

The sky streaking from the southwest
A fine hiss of the gas jet
The lamp overhead, rafters creaking

    Ideas that emerge one decade
End up like dead ants in the back room . . .

Roads that vanish into saplings.
A popular tune
Lying amongst tampax holders and sports
Periodicals

At the beach
Trout and perch driven high onshore
After such a sorry June
Winds and driving rain . . .

Something once populated with banter,
As one might say, to be generous about it

2.
    She enters from the bathroom
With a scent that seems beach-like,
A rustling of cottonwoods,
Unhooks and drops,
Then slips the other down

    Pushing through
A screen door

Sliding through the dew
The texture, the bias
The oscillations
The weight

Yes, the weight, interesting
The weight

Heather

Just as she was cruising through free traffic
A cop slammed into her chasing a drunk out of Arty's Place.
And you know Arty
Skirting this and that, they watch him.
With that gambling/dope/mob smoke.
Arty and Bam Bam: well she knows them through Steve
But wasn't heading there. Was Christmas shopping.
Now the Audi's demolished.
And that's another mouth to feed.
Never get what you goddamn want, not just exactly.
And that slug Arty, eats all his own food
Has to stand in front of a mirror just to see
What he's got. Ain't much, says Mickey.
But he's into spanking anyway.
Bam Bam won't say nothin' though.
Afraid or crazy.
Heather won't go in there without Bob

A New Restaurant

I was teasing
But I do that all the time when I'm not alone, he said
About the 3-some, I mean
My wife, another woman and me.
But, said his friend
In a 3-some
Isn't someone always a little neglected?

No, no you don't get the picture

I was at the next table
Greasy snow on bricks of the street
These tall wide windows
Pretending something on an empty street

It was not unpleasant

I could almost forget
My difficulties
And who I was supposed to meet

If I leaned back
I couldn't see the street at all

But shapes of older buildings at night
The way their owners once conceived them

Truth is, I wished I lived upstairs.

From another table there was talk regarding Tiffany
Who lost her finger in a door accident.
Well, they may have been able to reattach it
But the chocolate lab ate it before they thought to pick up the piece

Someone named Tony shook his head
Someone named Frank asked the gliding waitress how old she was
Someone else made a wager

At the bar
A woman who looked like a lawyer said
When the pancreas goes out, it's painful
You last about a day, day and a half

I decided to order

The New Neighbors

He said, in 1966 we shot out
All the streetlights
Between St. Ignace and Manistique
With a .22
From Cary's convertible

There's not that many, I said

More than you think, said the partner
From Howard, Howard, Smith and Howard

    Then, she said, I had this disagreement
With the band. Walked away in somewhere Pennsylvania.
Thought to myself, I ought to see NY.
Grabbed a bus, and the same day
Believe it or not, got a job as a singing waitress

Outside the sliding doors the wind was popping
With snow. We stopped by, I said,
To see what you were doing for New Years

You remember Cary Humphrey, he said
He sold the script for that new movie.
What the hell's it called

No, I said, I don't

    But I never did anything illegal,
She went on, I had a good time

It's odd how the years link up though
This project, this invention, that idea
That gift

The sad sour smell of memory, finally

What do you do now, my wife asked her

Transportation, she replied,

I sell light trucks at O'Hara Dodge.

Let's admit it, he said, truth has become overworked

Illness, desolation
The dog dead.
I much prefer these woods out back

All men are dicks, she said later
Not to me but my sister

Diebenkorn's *Ocean Park #52*

Every few years after the snow slipped away
There'd be a pond north of the granaries

In a depression so slight, a dent
So mirage-like in mist, listening to morning
Warm from eastern flatlands

In your jacket, near fence posts where chickens
Used to be, you'd wonder if anything was what
You thought it was. . .

In August riding a combine in the heat
(and in your sleep), leaden boundaries dissolving
It was sky, wheat, summerfallow and something
Else you'd grown attached to, that stillness
Of an old painting, the Lowlands of Holland

That nevertheless
Could suck the grit out of your pockets . . .

At horseshoes at night behind the bar in Gilford
In a useful daze, the sun settling like cheese
Dust of a pickup 60 years old, your heart
Bubbling softly in 1972, knowing when you reached home
Your slight blue would be there until winter

Saturday

Scent of the neighbor's wife
Hanging her underthings on the white line

Tied between the corner of the house
And a cherry tree in August

A female oriole flitting
To the sound of heartbeats from the cherry

Up to the elm from the channeled creek
Where its invisible nest droops

Like a jock-strap, as it will look in October
The interesting days of Indian summer

Awakening half-thoughts as she drove home
From the office and the sky so golden

She hitches her hip to the basket
Having doused herself with patchouli oil

And danced in North Beach unencumbered
Which is what she remembers

The humor, the attentions of the salesmen—
All the songbirds of the neighborhood

Won't change it either
Under their medieval sky she hums

With a clothespin in her mouth she hums
    In the center of her ripe yard

Birds Too

1.
Standing on the Indian Mound
In the park
Abe Lincoln
Had a high squeaky voice

Large grey birds
Circled about the steeples

2.
Following news on the economy
And civil strife
A local farmer says
"Deer are nothing but large rats"

He spits next to his boot
Chickens snap to attention

The reporter wishes he'd never
Gotten out of bed

3.
Lincoln said
"This mist will pass too"

In the flower beds
Tulips were arranged in red, white and bluish
Stripes. Gray squirrels raced
Between native chestnuts . . .

    Farther west
Grant stood below boundary pines
Hawks swinging lightly at the tops

Issues, he thought,
Are what we wrap fish in

4.
Newspapers dropped on the grass
Near benches
Where older teenagers exchange syringes

      Rats
Hunkering in bird feeders

      The sun breaking
Loose

      Towards dusk
Men walk back from the river
Fish tied to their belts

—you can't expect Television
to understand history

It's like the weather—

Just as birds
Come and go

5.
At night they roost in the woodlots
And abandoned steeples—

Maybe we make too much
Of cause and effect (anyway)

Misinterpret coincidence.

Grant saying
"There are small
Ratcheted tendons in a bird's toes
—keeps it from slipping while sleeping"

"It won't wake," joins Lincoln
His palms on the window
"Hanging upside down like an opossum"

Accountability

In wet snow
Tish tish of taillights
Seven deer
Wandering single-file
Up out of a gully.
You decide to pull off
Find a motel with an indoor pool
A bar and cable TV.

White birch, wild cherry
All day driving through the north—
Collapsing barns.
Those surprises
In the blankness of glass . . .

Sitting at dinner with sections of newspaper
Studying the report:
Bat dung
Festering in the heat, in the attic,
Caused the lodge to combust
In August . . .

Just about the time you think
You have nothing else to say,
Be bop, French ticklers, the Korean War . . .
Playing poker with visitors from
Georgia, ice fishing Carp Lake
With students from Indiana—
Fussing with sleep
You hear a train stammering west

Exiting miles off
From a trestle into wheat country.
Into the steaming silence.
Those dreams
Of attending the big university

No one would know you. Always
A new beginning.
Places where cemeteries
Are larger than the towns

        Hump of trees
        Across the lake
        Above the marsh

Mousy cupboards, bedsprings on porches
Getting screwed without a kiss,
Explained the matriarch—

The new casinos. Feral dogs.
The distress of families canoeing

On a warmer day.
Mist rising from culverts
Ears of hares—

Insects spanning the ripple
Of suds and sticks below—
Leaves cascading across highway 2

Two Parts

I was trying
To follow his story
Not moving my feet,
Studying a knot past
His shoulder in the wood
A door of this barn,
The blizzard outside
Forgotten temporarily,
The lady like the lady
On the illicit postcard.
How little I understood
What was profitable then.
Darts of snow in wind
Through a broken upper
Window, scent of straw,
Beams of trees scraped
And chiseled, boats
That were stored
Wrapped in green tarp,
The floor earthen
With 80 years
Of cow piss

*   *   *

I shook it off. Restless,
Drink in hand. A phrase,
A question, a cigarette,
Just as the trail grows
Colder on an idea you had.
The night particularly
Hesitant in a way, perhaps
It was the conversation.
Sinister metal sculptures.
Timbers. Windows deep-seated
In greyish-brown brick.
This renovated brewery
Now a home above a gallery.
Sturdy enough and dry.

A siren in the distance.
How the tin ceiling
Painted magenta seems
A good idea. How that morning,
Driving down Richmond Hill,
The shimmer of a factory roof
Resembled a pond's surface

How she looks so different
From the side, talking
To someone else

Coasts

My grandfather middle-aged and balding
Said it took them half a day
On a wagon from the farm

To Lake Michigan. Actually
The road ended before they got there

Had to climb a dune.
Smoking his cigar in a chair

Outside a motel in St. Ignace
His drink in a glass

Which, when tipped,
Showed a woman's clothes disappearing

She looked, I thought,
Much like a woman in the church choir—

He would go inside for ice
And whiskey. The cars on the road

Aiming for the ferry crossing
Until it was late, maybe too late

Appointments, plans,
Dubious anniversaries and celebrations

I got the point.

I liked waking to the paneling
In those rooms, too, the air

Pitched with voyaging, fish,
Wet rock and seaweed

Outside, a glimpse of water

My grandfather humming and shaving

At the sink in his T-shirt.

In the 1st World War
He was a fireman on a freighter

Heard the dud torpedoes
Smack the hull, those moments

When it snows in your head

A Town on the River

Handmade cribbage boards, oiled by fingers.
Creak of the chair, the plank
Resting on pine stumps . . .
The tourist congestion has left
Its complaints behind, amazing
How the sun breaks over the crowded hill
Of summer homes, only two pillars of smoke . . .
In the street a cement-mixer has a problem
Having slid past a wet corner and tumbled over,
Legs up in the air like a fat beetle,
Just a thud: the first time in a long while
Anyone looked at one closely.
On one of those redundant mornings
When the marching band is set up for its pomp
Through town—a few shopkeepers drinking coffee.
A wish of air and great sunlight.
The baker taking a smoke, his assistant taking a piss
In the alley. Even the gathering mallards
At the end of the street where the last fishing trawler
Is tied, and the street curves back towards the mill
Partly under water. Leaves in an eddy caused by breeze . . .
On the veranda the chairs and tables
Have been removed, the floor scrubbed and repainted.
The gallery has a sale—good luck to them.
Salmon have run up the sewers again
And into basements where they flop out
Near baskets of laundry. Other fish don't do that.
In the pie factory
It's the same situation. Too bad we don't
Make fish pies, says Ralph. And in the boat yard
Sandy sits in his office under a painting of his grandfather
Who left the orchard to work on the ferries. Sandy stares
Across the river sullen and sick at heart.
The water is wide here, gulls flap back and forth
Like a broken newsreel, squawk for the justice of it.
The only Indian in town sits in a rowboat wearing
A soiled down vest. He isn't too happy either.
A smear of sand like an interrupted paint job
On the upper slope,
A radio tower disturbs a bouncing tree-line of dune . . .

Whir of the sheriff's blinkered Ford racing from the beach
Through concaves of hardwood, where shanties once were.
Such dithering sounds of the high school marching band
Milling into the past, when promises were more advanced
When beachmen brought smoked perch to town . . .
Sugar maples in a fair-haired breeze, a woman
Tapping her foot in the phone booth
Scent of apple wood burning and leaves
Water nosing along the pavilion

Hairbrush

A woman's hairbrush, given to a boy
Who worships it, in his own fashion
Employs it on his own dark hair
Until the bristles are nubs
Still doesn't discard it, because,
Even though the scent has vanished
He senses her room and her at her table—
though he was never in it, never in the doorway,
even, but has developed the general features,
the subtle spunk—her used bed, her carpet,
A couple of framed photos of her family.

It was his first adult possession
Something to be hushed about, something
To be kept in his traveling bag.
Dark and mahogany-like, he could bring out,
All his own, several states away from home—
he kissed her neck, then smoothed
her hair—And oh, in the privacy of
His careful thoughts, across a sloping valley,
A woman's belly, flanks, a surface that
Moved on his own instructions.
Picturing her at her mirror, his fair hand,
His frankness, a brazenness equal to hers

Flies

He fidgets endless hours on Modernism
Tying it to Fascism, then returns—
The train backs up into realism
But it's not the depot it once was.
The wireless, for instance
Mothers dominating sons—General MacArthur
At West Point. Are his shorts clean?

What do you do with Symbolism
After all these years?
Is rain back to rain?
At his dusty sill he can't see the fire for the drought.
Is it the sun lying flat on the water? His wife
Smoking dope with the neighbor? His son butchering the lamb?
No one knows where the depot used to be.

The Snakes

In the cabin
Snakes have eaten the mice.
They stretch among fingers
Of kindling under the barrel stove.
Some days I feed them
Grasshoppers.
Some days
Hamburger on a toothpick.
At night
They slide beneath the floor.
Flies hatch from mud
Under the cabin.
I've used the mouse-traps
To balance the table, the counter
And the bunk.
In the morning
A woodpecker rivets the peak.
I still need to paint it.
Getting up
To make a fire, brush my teeth.
Outside
Smoke hovers
In a bank that widens.
I pee on a frosty stand
Of milkweed.
Leaves of the appletree
Hang loosely.
Through the open door
The snakes study me

Brick

The one I liked best
Called my paintbrush
A feather—heat rattling
Through the radiators
A whiff of soiled diapers.
A map of the world
I'm lifting from the wall.
I want my red rooster
She says, licking her spoon.
Let's eat our own shit
Says her roommate.
But neither is talking
To anyone in particular

Wind skirts the alley
With sparks of snow.
The sound of back-hoes
Digging to frozen pipe—
Gigantic horses' hoofs.
They're coming to rescue us
From this whorehouse
She says, rising from bed . . .
I've grown strangely fond
Of the rungs and chutes
Of the Alzheimer's unit . . .

You have a dog's face
Says her roommate, you are
All dogs without hope

Across the brick street
An agent for the featherweight
Fighter, wiping up the last
Of his mushrooms and sauce
Suggests that ticket sales
Have been proceeding nicely.
His suit blending with
The woodwork and plaques

My reddish ale—in the mirror
An idling bus at the door

Steam vents and snow, blisters
Of snow and city ash.
Where is my baby, she asked.
My baby can walk, my baby
Can walk

The Focus

So in the room
She unfastens herself
From an 800 dollar business suit
Almost afraid I won't notice

I try not to
Changing the channels
From the bed until she closes
The door to the bathroom
A faucet singing

And it's true
I'm reminded of football,
Though I lived for the feints
The particles, the piling up
Of tendencies, granted I was
Seldom correct, anticipating
Let's say, the end-around

But the focus, a calmness in focus,
On a mile of green
While the stadium went berserk.
I was the one chess piece
That couldn't be trusted
Which was the beauty of my position

Those white rollers
Of anticipation—anyway,
Coached well or not,
Everyone else my size
Was eventually injured

Night

1.
The clown runs in.
It's difficult to tell
How much dope he'd smoked.
But this is what he
Races for

2.
In the little trailer
Ensconced in mud
We hear the rain
Clearly enough. In Canada
All the talk is of winter
In Florida

3.
The clown transforms.
He is hungry now.
We all knew him in High School.
The boss's wife has wild red hair.
She likes us as we are.
The elephant is pulling at its stake.
There is gambling
Down the line
Where lights of the fairground
Are aging

4.
In the next trailer
Gin is being served.
Do we go to town or not?
And who drives?
The boss's wife laughs like a virgin
Causes the clown to stutter.
Maybe his life was doomed from the start.

Outside we stand in mud
The heavens spiraling down
With tiny shots of lead.
You can smell the ocean, he says

5.
We can't. But we don't care
Anyway. In the inn
He will surreptitiously
Eat all the guppies in the tank behind us.
The boss's wife will grow more shapely.
In Florida no one thinks he's queer
He says. The locals
Will stare, amused, but he is in a mist now
And can't believe in reason

6.
The boss's wife holds his hand.
None of us are hopeful.
We say, Bay of Fundy, Prince Edward Island,
Port aux Basques. We don't want
The son-of-a-bitch to cry.
He tries to keep from vomiting

>   To distract him
>   We open the door
>   On the road home
>   To hit a mile of mailboxes

We are impoverished, he says.
But his nose is clear. We rock
Through the puddles.
That's better, that's better
She says

Phillip

From the site of the murder
It's a mushrooming process
The farther he's traveled.
Distance and time
Have their own accelerators.
He's moved by the sparrows
Of the lawn, the vining fence
To contemplate new paradigms
And techniques of surveillance—

Lying for hours in the dark
Letting everything grow
Just as he grows, the figure
In the dollhouse, the squeaks
And rustlings of growth, busting
Out finally into a naked sunshine

Poor Phillip wasn't prepared
Blinking like a miner, arms large
And flabby, running his hand
Over and over down the left side
Of his face. But there he is
Fully awake for light, stopping to tie
His long hair like his mother did hers.
Soon he will have to move on—
There may be some hope in North Dakota.
He has heard from unnamed acquaintances
The mutterings of proof. Instead
Of the tics and hops of logic
Termite trails of reason run amok
A lively clean air of individuality.
Dryness. Resolutions, in short,
Of bird song and honeyed horizon
Spilling out across the carpet,
Bare farmhouse carpet—

Vapors of the past, this hell,
This repository, where noodlings
Of criminal ties, networks of minutia
And lies, where the impossible

Turns into the hoofs and muzzles
Of deceit. You see what I'm painting here
Having to travel at night
In this old woman's coat and scarf
Not knowing where the grief spreads out
Flat and plain. Where the cold blood of
Drowning just vanishes down a rathole.
Where hell greets a larger more graphic hell
You tell me, I've got 68 hundred pages
Of evidence, and you can kiss my butt
If you think I'm going back to prison, he said

Families

Who can forget
The dried leaves skipping across the patio.
Mother says, you were a difficult birth.
Grandmother says the same about her
Though the latter took place on a kitchen table.
Outside, men smoked cigars
Felt sick but didn't show it.
One feels distanced by the black shoes
Of old women. But in photographs
The shoes look good when the women were twenty.
All the trees were young too.
As they walk down a hard-baked lane.
Only the men look odd.
Strangers, mostly.
Mother says, you can have all that stuff
We're going away.
Grandmother says, yes,
I was always a Progressive. Then all
The men died young. One shouldn't forget
That everyone got cheated somehow.
Mother is going to Palm Springs.
Dad is going fishing. He was
A difficult birth too.

Who can forget those long evenings
Drinking port talking about grandfather.
He was a real worker. He was a corker
Says grandmother.
Mother says, I hate Spring,
It reminds me of being poor.
It reminds me of being old, says grandmother,
But no one is paying attention now.
I *had* to get married, she adds.

One sits under the tree where picnics once were.
Beetles and sand fleas.
All of them seated
Complexions like peaches
The sun shaking through the cottonwoods
Patterns of leaves snaking through sand.

Or the new wood sidings of homes
When cemeteries were what you had to cross
In order to get to the country

Outside of Town

1.
Lou Gehrig's disease
Is caused by a bad diet
And drinking diet pop
She said, at the next table

With a grey sky
Melting over the windows
Like bankruptcy

2.
Spring training
In Florida,
Pulled stomach muscles
Stolen wallet and clothes—

A red truck
In a field of disappointment

The staghorn tufts of sumac
Battered by birds and weather

I told you, she said,
Tax time is no time
To be hiring

Life goes on, her male friend noted

Some are lucky to be lucky
She said finally
Standing, fooling in her purse

Up North

The breeze brings a fragrance
Of youthfulness

All the animals are hiding

I would like to hide too

Such is the Windemere
Of our spirits and deeds sometimes

That overwhelming hangover
Of regret
That rides down like a giant sliver
With leaves and small twigs

There's nothing to do
But complain

(shoot complain
in the knees
and it still hobbles)

What conclusions
Do you want me to draw?

That it is self-defeating
To ignore the trees?

Myself, I prefer white pine

In May

1.
I guess my idea
Is different than yours

And your wife too
Flicking at some bug

On her breast,
In a bulky Michigan sweatshirt

      It wasn't me after all
Who went after you

I was minding my own work

And yes, it was
Like October
In a funny way

But not quite, I mean
There was a difference in the sky

      I was sure
I understood
What I'd missed earlier

But no one would agree
With me, not these days

2.
The trouble with Out West
Is there aren't enough trees
Or they're the wrong kind
He said

I'm afraid
I was staring at that bug

The white pine when young
Are terribly feminine,
He continued

3.
Nothing left
But pee in the grass

The sun is there,
Kind of a surprise—

Some Persian love poem
Messed up in translation

4.
But I am not in charge, I thought,
Of kindness

Deceptions either . . .

       The maples looking tall
And vigorous, the frost
Gone out of the soil just then . . .

Veterans

In her wedding dress
Or maybe a borrowed one.
What's the difference.
The man comes in, perhaps
Forcefully, a sailor no doubt,
Or some professional student
Masquerading as one, yeah,
Yeah, the seats squeal . . .
Though poets too are writing
Energetic lines, a chemical engineer
Sees perfection, flags are unfurled . . .
In the war, the bomber mechanic says,
Fuck, the fucken fucker's fucked.
Well, she spends the better part
Of an hour with the dress over her face
And is not, it seems, terrified or unhappy.
Rather, it is just the thing
To take her mind off weighty and niggling events.
The audience understands
They've seen it a thousand times.
It's that moment added to moment they all cherish.
An episode that ends up misunderstood however
In the long run of experience

The Cottonwoods

A plane trailing a message over water
Where women stroll at the edge of waves looking up

Once when you were 14, the seeds caught fire.
That scum of white among the ground vines. Wild grape
And Virginia creeper—

Stark light in the grasses, light in the sand.
Growing cool and wanting you. Where your thoughts don't change—

Bathe in waves and nestle down, like an Indian
Awaiting the French priests . . .

Men in sweat-soaked robes
Wading ashore

Beach birds and shadow. The smoke.
The narcotic waves of smoke. Starkness of ashes

High in the canopy where you might have concealed yourself
But didn't

Summer of '94

1.
My legs were sore from swimming

When I got up
Trish was already in the shower.
I had a moment to feel old
That clap of a hand
On my shoulder

2.
We were reading the latest polls
In an out-of-town paper

The waitress refilled our coffees.
Are you voters? she asked

Yeah. I nodded.

As she bobbed away
I realized
She'd actually said "boaters"

Trish looked up, why did you say that?

How would she know, I said.
But I was still thinking

Of an acquaintance
Who was running for governor

We were sitting outside
On a fashionable deck

Above a marshy estuary
Swans and geese in the sun, boats of bass fishermen

Across the water
Reeds had been removed, the muck

Hauled up
A marina jammed an entire Sunday morning

Pass the jelly, said Trish

3.
That evening we walked
Through the shopping district.
A harmless town.
Spell of the marsh and idling water
Main Street curved
Slipped over the bridge.
Occasional scent of the big lake
Dropping in and mingling.
The beach wasn't many miles
Away.

It's true, I said, I haven't seen him
In twenty-five years. He's pudgier
In the picture.
He's one of the gang though
I used to sell dope to
A couple of times a week

Breath

1.
Your breath cutting a hole in the air
Hawks circling

All day gathering firewood

Until the sky is another face.
One sensation
Bleeding into the moss of something else.
Rattle of beech leaves.
Silence of mud

With hips of another moment
Moving through this room
The open door

You rest against the door
On a yellow kitchen chair

2.
    Wouldn't it be useful to be a wise man
In old age, rather than twitching like a bat in daylight . . .

    That coil around the sun

    Cattle at a friendly pace
Turning into a weathered wind.
Right there
At some piling exposed, this faint
Abscess running up the knoll

3.
There have always been antique dealers,
We know. In Rome
They were particularly popular

4.
Keep pulling
The shroud on an ancient mummy
Until you end up
Where you don't want to be.

>   Margy said,
>   I hate that song.
>
>   You've got to take her at her word.

>   It's like working
For the common good.

At home
With a breeze shopping through the willows.
Or in the country. Leaning on a post left by loggers

>   Why cheapen yourself
Like a literary whore

5.
Watching a leaf walk
Across the ground, until you realize
It's a mouse or shrew
Carrying the leaf on its back
To fold down a tiny burrow along the path
Re-emerging to carry another.

In the sky at night
Major holes among the constellations

Hired Hand

How bawdy the warmth
A current, stones underfoot,
The scent of movement, a melody
That hooks it, until arguments
Begin among drunks
Under shadows of western trees
Outside the bar, I don't remember,
(Box Elder?), climbing steps
In that vast darkness and distance.
How roads give out near piles
Of rocks and ghostly machinery.
I was none too sober either,
A daydreamer, finicky for my age.
It was like a phone ringing
That no one would answer, shifting
To an available corner of calm
Which won't stay put

Beetles

Two black beetles copulating
On a mound of earth
An extinguished ant hill
Behind the motel cabin—
I carried a thermos and camera.
The woman who owned the place
Described a trail to the petroglyphs

      After light rain
Fiddlehead fern
Unscrolling

*   *   *

He hit a moose on 41
Sheared the top of the Taurus
Him too. Is that a problem
In these parts now, I asked.
Naw. He's the first. Wiping
His hands on a red rag

Neighbors

The wind spins suddenly, leaves chattering.
Richard disappearing in smoke

Into a meadow of time, only to reappear coughing

Life sucks, says Kent, examining his fingers

But I was thinking of my Dad back from the office
Bathing in the lake with a bar of soap

Scent of a cooking roast curling down the walk

My mother, in a print dress
Desiring more order in the vagaries of nature

Or myself, at twelve, concocting erotic plans
For women like Doris, the perfume of skin

The planes and venetian blinds of abandonment—

Kent stumping down the stairs, accidentally
Dropping his keys into rocks by the flowers

Waves chunking into the seawall

Once

The man had a brown caterpillar
On his shirt
I said is this your friend
He looked down
No he said
This is my son

We walked on
The wind in the northern forest
Seemed full of Biblical quotations
Small red squirrels
Scattered in front of us

My brother finally said
I'm sorry
We have to go home now

We were standing by one of the old logs
We were both hungry

The man was sad
He fired his shotgun
Into the sky
Only leaves came down

We turned

Stop he said

We went on walking
Through dead leaves
(we were both afraid
he might shoot us)

Come home with me
He pleaded
I will introduce you to a woman

Elm Ridge Street

That rabbit smell at the fence
The dog understands

While you spot a neighbor
Unzipping his pants

To urinate behind his ash

A free lot between you.
All the men

Are watching football inside
Or napping with their wives

It's embarrassing
When he sees you

Of course the dog is trying
To undo the fence—

A worm in the guts

Trying to make a long rope
Out of knots

Perhaps his mate
Is pouring whiskey

Into the sink
His underwear out a front window.

Blackberry vines
Concealing mounds

Of shoveled soil.
Contractor's trash

A warren of tunnels.
Bad rumors.

Your dog whines
Fumbles back and forth—

Maybe he missed deer camp
This year

His portfolio is dying

From an upper window
His son cries Dad

The Painting

Where a farmer switches a cow
Along a path to water
Ships are moored a ways out

A prosperous time
Before detritus. Certain rules
Still intact
Involving partnerships in commerce
And basic intelligence

One wouldn't say,
Hide, Martha!
Here come the damn potlickers

Or worse, as the decades deteriorated—

Nobody had to hide
It was quite the opposite

No one even closed their curtains

      An earthiness
Still extant
Kept Calvinists in check

It wasn't restricted to taverns
Bawdy playwrights, insecure investors

That is, you got a free salted herring
With your ale

Or oysters or smoked chubs

Drawing rooms were similar

The whole company guffawing
The burgher's wife leaning over your shoulder

      Landscape painters

Woke the next day, splashed their faces

Ate their rusk, smiled at their children

        Or how the sparrow waits
Until the sweeping is accomplished

All the porches swept, the conversations
Salutations, the walks swept

Then has no hesitation

        —Just as the cow's eye
remains perfectly focused
but the farmer isn't

        or the hardy hedge
the squatting beech, a security of green.
This mound to stand on, this terp,
where something was once erected,
rotted away

        whereas the ships
        float high
        the sky is tranquil
        the fish teem unseen
        and so forth—

Reeds playing the bank. A broken tree branch.
Swish of a tail. Cow pies
In the leaning grasses.
Some cottage deep in the distance
A dab of blue and red. A marsh scent

        —Where we could go
You and I. Mind our own business.
Drink all the chocolate we wanted.
I could smoke a pipe at the end
Of day. Look out.

At the spires and rigging . . .

        You might, she said,
Be over-reacting

Prints in a cheap art book
For godsakes. Golden Age nonsense.
These popping little holes of silence, you say.
Crowsfeet of silence is more like it

These towns where the gossip never quits

I don't care how deep
In the marsh you live

Acknowledgements

Versions of these poems have appeared in the following magazines:

Artful Dodge: "Saturday," "Outside of Town"

B-City: "Coasts"

Brief: "The Cottonwoods"

Caliban: "Flies"

Carbuncle: "Heather"

Cincinnati Poetry Review: "Once"

Epoch: "The Snakes," "The Focus," "Neighbors"

Giants Play Well in the Drizzle: "Hairbrush," "Families," "Veterans"

Grand Street: "Bodies," "Detail"

Green River Review: "Once"

House Organ: "Monotony," "Breath," "The Painting"

Jejune: "A New Restaurant," "The New Neighbors," "Birds Too"

Parnassus: "The Brightness," "Showtime," "A Town on the River"

The Regulator: "In May"

Sulfur: "Up North," "Elm Ridge Street"

"Once," "The Cottonwoods," "Hairbrush," "Veterans," and "Saturday" also appeared in *Peaches*, SkyBooks, 1998.

"Cricket Poem" originally appeared in *Circumstances*, The Sumac Press, 1978.

"Bodies," and "Outside of Town" appeared in *New Poems from the Third Coast*, Wayne State University Press, 2000.

"Summer of '94" appeared in *The Talking of Hands*, New Rivers Press, 1998.

"Diebenkorn's Ocean Park #52" appeared in *A Visit to the Gallery*, University of Michigan Press, 1997.

"Up North" appeared in *Contemporary Michigan Poetry*, Wayne State University Press, 1988.

"Night" appeared in *Night Weather*, Northern Lights Press, 1991.

photo by Deb VanderMolen

Robert VanderMolen has been publishing poems in such periodicals as *Caliban*, *Cincinnati Poetry Review*, *Epoch*, *Grand Street*, *Parnassus*, and *Sulfur*, since the mid-1960's. After receiving degrees from Michigan State University and the University of Oregon, he taught at the Community College in Grand Rapids, Michigan, before drifting into business as a painting contractor. He was awarded an NEA Fellowship in 1995. Previous collections of poetry include *Peaches* (SkyBooks), *Circumstances*, and *The Pavilion* (both from Sumac Press). As a rule, four times a year he heads up to a cabin in the Upper Peninsula of Michigan for extended stays. VanderMolen lives with his wife and two sons in Grand Rapids, Michigan.

New Issues Poetry & Prose

Editor, Herbert Scott

James Armstrong, *Monument in a Summer Hat*
Anthony Butts, *Fifth Season*
Gladys Cardiff, *A Bare Unpainted Table*
Lisa Fishman, *The Deep Heart's Core Is a Suitcase*
Joseph Featherstone, *Brace's Cove*
Robert Grunst, *The Smallest Bird in North America*
Edward Haworth Hoeppner, *Rain Through High Windows*
Josie Kearns, *New Numbers*
Lance Larsen, *Erasable Walls*
David Dodd Lee, *Downsides of Fish Culture*
Deanne Lundin, *The Ginseng Hunter's Notebook*
Joy Manesiotis, *They Sing to Her Bones*
David Marlatt, *A Hog Slaughtering Woman*
Paula McLain, *Less of Her*
Malena Mörling, *Ocean Avenue*
Julie Moulds, *The Woman With a Cubed Head*
Marsha de la O, *Black Hope*
C. Mikal Oness, *Water Becomes Bone*
Margaret Rabb, *Granite Dives*
Rebecca Reynolds, *Daughter of the Hangnail*
Martha Rhodes, *Perfect Disappearance*
John Rybicki, *Traveling at High Speeds*
Mark Scott, *Tactile Values*
Diane Seuss-Brakeman, *It Blows You Hollow*
Marc Sheehan, *Greatest Hits*
Phillip Sterling, *Mutual Shores*
Angela Sorby, *Distance Learning*
Russell Thorburn, *Approximate Desire*
Robert VanderMolen, *Breath*
Martin Walls, *Small Human Detail in Care of National Trust*
Patricia Jabbeh Wesley, *Before the Palm Could Bloom: Poems of Africa*